581

BASEBALL:
IT'S YOUR TEAM

Nate Aaseng

 Lerner Publications Company ▪ Minneapolis

To Mikhaila

LIBRARY OF CONGRESS CATALOGING IN PUBLICATION DATA

Aaseng, Nathan.
  Baseball, it's your team.

  Summary: Presents ten crucial situations major league
baseball team owners have had to face, permitting the
reader to make the decision from reading the facts.
  1. Baseball—United States—Miscellanea—Juvenile
literature. [1. Baseball—Miscellanea. 2. Baseball—
Team owners] I. Title
GV867.5.A17   1985   796.357'64'0973   84-28918
ISBN 0-8225-1558-X (lib. bdg.)

  2   3   4   5   6   7   8   9   10   94   93   92   91   90   89   88   87   86

CONTENTS

It's Your Baseball Team!

Do you get upset when your favorite baseball team falls into a slump that lasts from Memorial Day until Labor Day? Does it bother you when the hotshot your team signed for $4 million hobbles around on crutches all season? Is it exciting to find out that your team has finally traded for that shortstop who could help them win the pennant?

Imagine how it would feel, then, if you actually owned the team. Suddenly much more would be at stake than simply your entertainment. Your money, your pride, and your reputation, as well as the hopes of millions of fans, would be riding on your every move.

You are about to join one of the most exclusive clubs in the United States: the club of major league baseball owners. As you try to outdeal and outwit some of the most famous and powerful people in the country, you'll be mixing in some pretty fast company. Baseball owners have traditionally been more active and outspoken in

5

running their teams than owners of teams in other sports. People such as George Steinbrenner of the Yankees and Ted Turner of the Braves have often made more headlines than their players. Former Padres owner Ray Kroc once grabbed a microphone in the middle of a home game to blast his players for poor play. Another former owner, Calvin Griffith, probably stirred up more criticism than anyone else in the state of Minnesota as he guided his Minnesota Twins.

Although there are some owners who have preferred to pass on the job of running the club to a general manager, many others such as Charlie Finley, Phil Wrigley, Bill Veeck, August Busch, and Walter O'Malley have often stepped in to take matters into their own hands.

It may be a bit unsettling for you to realize that the very mention of an owner's name can provoke boos in most ball parks. Fans have little patience with someone who makes a mistake with "their" team. If you can't pull your team out of a five-year stay at the bottom of the standings, fans are sure to take out their frustrations on you. If you trade away your top player for a pitcher who turns out to have a sore arm, they'll be howling for your hide. If you don't find a way to patch up a weak spot on your team in the middle of a pennant race, they'll want to know why.

Ten crucial decisions await your judgment in this book. With just a nod of your head you can lose a million dollars, capture a World Series title, or destroy an entire franchise. How will you handle the power that comes with owning your own team?

1 Speed vs. Power

You own the New York Yankees.

After your stinging defeat at the hands of the Los Angeles Dodgers in the 1981 World Series, you've been groping for answers as to what went wrong. Some critics have suggested that your team needs more speed in the field and on the basepaths.

Traditionally your Yankees have relied on power and pitching rather than on speed for their wins. In order to get more speed in your lineup, you may have to sacrifice some of that power. How many home runs are you willing to give up in exchange for a faster team?

Consider which speedsters from other teams might be available to you.

The Cincinnati Reds have a couple of swift players who could be yours for almost nothing. One of them is right fielder Ken Griffey. One of the most underrated players in the game, Griffey has quietly batted over .300 in five of his seven seasons as a regular. He can cover a lot of ground in the outfield and has averaged 20 stolen bases per year during his career. Yet the cash-poor Reds are willing to trade him and his high salary to you for a couple of low budget minor league players.

The other man is outfielder-first baseman Dave Collins. Although he tailed off last year to a still-respectable .272 average, Collins is also capable of hitting over .300, as he showed in both 1979 and 1980. Collins stole 79 bases in 1980, which established him as one of the fastest men in the game. The best news about Collins is that he is a free agent, so you could get him without having to give up any of your players in trade. In the past you have had no trouble outbidding other teams for free agents.

Ken Griffey   Dave Collins

Now consider which of your starters these men would replace.

You already have more outfielders than you need. Dave Winfield, the highest-paid player in the game, patrols left field, while .307-hitting Jerry Mumphrey anchors your defense in center field. If Griffey comes in to take over right field and Collins moves to first base, that leaves Reggie Jackson, Oscar Gamble, Lou Piniella, and Bob Watson scrambling for the designated hitter position and any leftover playing time. All are proven big-league hitters who won't be happy sitting on the bench all year.

It would be easiest to get rid of Jackson. He is currently a free agent and may be in a position to ask for more money than you want to give him. If Collins and Griffey join the team, you might not need Reggie because you would already have a left-handed, power-hitting reserve in Oscar Gamble.

You couldn't ask for much more from outfielders Jerry Mumphrey (top left) and Dave Winfield (bottom left). In right field, however, there seems to be a logjam of slow-footed sluggers such as Oscar Gamble (above).

Reggie, however, is not a player you can treat lightly. A colorful, popular player, Jackson has long been one of the top home-run hitters in the game. Just two years ago he led the American League with 41 home runs while hitting .300 for the first time in his career. A proven clutch hitter, Jackson has drilled 10 home runs in World Series action, including 3 in one game back in 1977. He has won a lot of games for your Yankees and would prefer to stay with New York.

Reggie Jackson's clutch postseason home runs have earned him the nickname "Mr. October." But you have to sacrifice defense to get his bat in the lineup.

On the other hand, Reggie will be 36 years old this year and is coming off a bad season. Even with a late-season spurt, he still only batted .237 with 15 home runs last year. He is not a base stealer and is certainly not known for his defense. With Winfield, Watson, Gamble, and Craig Nettles around, your Yankees would still have home run power without him.

What's Your Decision?

It's your team. You want another chance at the World Series title next year.
What changes, if any, will you make for the 1982 season?

#1 Acquire Griffey and Collins. Also sign Jackson.

#2 Acquire Griffey and Collins. Let Jackson go.

#3 Sign Jackson and stay with the players you have. Don't go after Griffey and Collins.

Choose your strategy. Then turn the page to see what the Yankees did.

The Yankees went with choice #2.

Deciding that they really needed more team speed, New York felt they could not pass up the chance to get Griffey and Collins so cheaply. But they did not want to be saddled with a bench full of unhappy ex-stars. Yankee owner George Steinbrenner, after consulting with his baseball experts, decided that the Yankees could win without Jackson. Therefore, he decided to acquire the two Reds and make no effort to sign Reggie.

Here's What Happened!

The Yankees' new strategy of speed over power backfired in 1982. Griffey and Collins added little to the offense as they hit poorly and combined for only 23 stolen bases. Griffey's average fell to .277, and Collins hit so poorly (.253 with only 3 home runs) that he was sold to Toronto the next year. The Yankees' production of runs fell off so badly that the defending American League champions wound up with a losing record (79-83), their worst finish since 1967.

Jackson, meanwhile, signed with the California Angels. The veteran slugger enjoyed a fine season as he helped hoist the Angels from a losing record in 1981 to the American League West title.

Jackson smashes another well-hit piece of evidence to prove that the Yankees blew it. New York badly needed the league-leading 39 home runs and 101 runs batted in that Reggie gave the Angels in 1981.

2 Deadline for a Deal

Rod Carew is threatening to take his bat and go to another team, and there's not much you can do about it.

You own the Minnesota Twins.

Your low-budget team is struggling to find a way to compete with the wealthier clubs in the American League. Sensing that the Twins are facing a bleak future and that they could make more money elsewhere, your stars are bailing out. The latest to announce that he will no longer play for Minnesota is your biggest star of all, Rod Carew. Carew has said that if he is not traded to another team, he will play out his option this year and become a free agent.

As the 1979 season approaches, you're trying hard to make a good trade involving Carew. But your star player has two demands which are making things even more difficult. First, he's given you a deadline for completing a deal. If a satisfactory trade isn't made within two days, Carew will play out his option. Secondly, he's made it clear that he will only accept a trade to one of a select group of ball clubs. Your job is to salvage something out of the situation.

Consider what will happen if you don't take any action.

If you don't give Carew what he wants, you will lose one of baseball's most popular stars without getting a thing in return. Carew will play out his option. In other words, he will fulfill his contract with the Twins by playing for you in 1979 and will be free to offer his future services to the highest bidder.

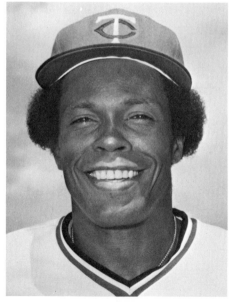

Part of Rod Carew's frustration as a Twin is the fact that he has never been able to play in a World Series.

During the past couple of years, you've already lost a solid group of ballplayers without any compensation. Relief pitchers Bill Campbell and Tom Burgmeier, sluggers Larry Hisle and Eric Soderholm, and .300-hitting outfielder Lyman Bostock have all left for greener pastures. You didn't get a cent or a player in return.

Carew should bring a good price in a trade because he is such a valuable player. Even during an "off-year" in 1978, Carew's .333 batting average was still good enough to lead the American League. That was the seventh batting championship in the past 10 years for the amazing Rodney. It kept his career average at .334, far above that of any other veteran now in the game. (Even Pete Rose has managed only .310.) Although not famous for his fielding, Carew has developed into a capable first baseman since switching to that position from second base in 1975.

Just two seasons ago Carew showed his value by flirting with the magic .400 mark. Posting the best major league batting mark since Ted Williams hit .388 back in 1957, Carew's .388 average brought him — and your Twins —national publicity. A player of his caliber wins games for his team, and, even more importantly, draws out the fans.

Now look over your options in the trading market.

Carew hasn't left you in a good position for a trade. You had already worked out a trade with the San Francisco Giants two months ago, only to have Carew veto the deal. Then you thought you had something worked out with the New York Yankees. The Yankees backed off when their owner, George Steinbrenner, became miffed over Rod's reluctance to join his team. As a 12-year veteran, Carew has the right to decline any trade you might make.

That really leaves the California Angels as the only serious bidder for Rod's services. Aware that Rod would like to join them and that there is little competition in the bidding, they are offering less than they otherwise might. They have refused to give you the man you would like in exchange, Carney Lansford. Instead they have offered four young and unproven players:

1. Pitcher **Paul Hartzell**, a right-hander who won 6 and lost 10 for the Angels last year with a 3.44 earned run average.

2. Outfielder **Ken Landreaux**, a speedster who hit spectacularly in the minor leagues but batted only .223 in his first full year as an Angel.

3. Outfielder **Dave Engle**, a 22-year old who is several years away from being ready for a chance at big-league pitching.

4. Pitcher **Brad Havens**, who, at the age of 19, shows exceptional maturity and promise.

The Angels are also including $200,000 in the deal, money which your penny-pinching franchise could use.

Paul Hartzell

Ken Landreaux

In making the trade, you would be gambling that these youngsters would make it in the majors. Back in 1976 you took a similar chance when you traded away disgruntled star pitcher Bert Blyleven. Two of the young players you received in the trade, Roy Smalley, Jr., and Mike Cubbage, have developed into starters for you. If the same thing happens this time, you might be as well off rebuilding with these young players than with the 33-year old Carew.

Considering how little California is offering, you might gain more by hanging on to Carew for one more year.

A superstar like Carew should command a higher price than what the Angels are offering. You don't have to take their offer; you could "rent" Carew for a year. To rent a star, teams keep or trade for a player who is playing out his option. That way, for a reduced price, they get the services of the player for one year before he becomes a free agent. The Baltimore Orioles got one year out of Reggie Jackson in 1976 with this technique. The next season the White Sox tried the same thing and got a fine season out of Richie Zisk.

In 1976 the Baltimore Orioles traded for Reggie Jackson even though the slugger was playing out his option and would be a free agent at the end of the year. Jackson gave the Orioles 27 homers and 91 RBI's before moving on to the Yankees.

If you let Carew play out his option, you would get his services for one year at a salary of $180,000. During a time when even unproven players draw $100,000 salaries, that's a huge bargain. Considering that Carew would be pushing for a big year to increase his bargaining power as a free agent, he may give you more for your money in one year than what the Angels are offering.

What's Your Decision?

It's your team.
Carew has made it clear that he will not sign another contract with the Twins. You have just two days to decide what to do. What will it be?

#1 Make the trade.
#2 Let Carew play out his option.

Choose your strategy. Then turn the page to see what the Twins' owner did.

The Twins went with choice #1.

It was obvious from Carew's demands that he was not happy with the Twins. In that situation, the Twins felt that everyone would be better off if Carew were traded. After the number of free agents Twins owner Calvin Griffith had already lost, he was under pressure to get *something* for Carew. While not thrilled with what the Angels were offering, Griffith decided it was the best choice available to him.

Here's What Happened!

Carew continued to batter American League pitching for his new team. He immediately helped California to the American League West title in 1979 and did so again in 1982. During his next five seasons following the trade, his batting average never dipped below .300.

The Twins, meanwhile, gradually lost whatever respect they still had from their fans and opponents. Ken Landreaux tried to make up for Carew's loss with a .305 mark in 1979, as the Twins fought gamely to finish at 82-80. But first Hartzell and then Havens failed in their bids to become effective pitchers. Engle struggled at the plate, and Landreaux was traded to the Dodgers before the 1981 season as the Twins scraped bottom in both wins and attendance in 1981 and 1982.

Carew made things happen for the Angels on the base paths as well as at the plate.

Sometimes, though, it takes several years before the final verdict is in on a deal. In 1983, five years after the trade was made, it began to pay off for the Twins. Mickey Hatcher, the outfielder they received from the Dodgers for Landreaux, batted .317 with 9 home runs. Dave Engle batted .305 with 8 homers that year and began a successful switch to the position of catcher. Engle, who made the American League All-Star team in 1984, and Hatcher were two key ingredients of the Twins' amazing challenge for the 1984 American League West title.

Had Carew played out his option with the Twins, his hitting would have been wasted on a very weak team. Instead, the Twins were able to take a bad situation and work out a deal that helped them rebuild their club.

Although he's no Rod Carew at the plate, Mickey Hatcher eased the pain of Carew's leaving. The Carew trade eventually gave the Twins two key players in their 1984 pennant challenge that fell only a few games short of a divisional title.

3 The Price of Success

Bruce Sutter is making a salary pitch that is just as baffling as his famous split-fingered fastball.

You own the Chicago Cubs.

Your team hasn't had much to brag about over the past 35 years. The Cubs haven't won a pennant since 1945, and only a smattering of All-Star players have worn a Cub uniform since then.

But now it's 1980, and your team is led by one of the hottest young pitchers in the game, Bruce Sutter. Based on his performance in 1979, Sutter may be not only the best reliever in the National League but also the most valuable pitcher in baseball.

While you have been enjoying Sutter's success, you also realize that it could be very expensive for you. Your star pitcher thinks that he should collect about $700,000 a year for his efforts. There isn't a National League pitcher making close to that amount of money right now. With only four years of experience, Sutter would be at the top of the salary scale. How will you handle the situation?

Consider Sutter's value to your club.

Bruce Sutter's specialty pitch, the split-fingered fastball, has become the toughest pitch to hit in baseball. Since no other pitcher has mastered it, batters never see this fast-dropping pitch at any other time and have no chance to practice against it.

After offering a preview of what he could do in 1976, Bruce went on to post astounding records the next season. In 107 innings, he allowed only 69 hits while striking out 129 for an unbelievable earned run average of 1.35. Sutter's performance in 1978 was less impressive, but he made up for it in 1979 with a spectacular season. He gave up just 67 hits in 101 innings and tied a National League record by saving 37 games. Bruce handcuffed opponents so completely that he became one of the few relief pitchers ever to win the Cy Young Award as his league's top pitcher.

It often takes several years of experience for a pitcher to handle the pressure of late-inning relief pitching. But Sutter will be only 27 this season and, if he stays healthy, can look forward to more than a decade of mastery on the mound.

Next, check out the brief history of salary arbitration.

If Sutter does not agree to your contract terms, and it looks as if he won't, he will take the matter to binding arbitration. This system, which was introduced to baseball in the past few years, brings in a third party to decide the salary. The player names the figure he thinks he deserves, and the team names the figure they think he deserves. The arbitrator then chooses the figure he or she thinks is most fair. There can be no compromise or choosing a number in between; the arbitrator must choose either your figure or Sutter's.

The arbitration system does not seem to heavily favor one side over the other. Players, however, have tended to win more cases than they have lost. Last year there were twelve disputes brought to arbitration. The players won eight times, the owners won four. Among pitchers, four players won and two lost. In the cases of the pitchers, the players and owners were not that far apart in their figures. The greatest difference between a player's demand and a team's offer was $38,000. That was in the case of California's Dyar Miller, who lost his case. Neither Miller, though, nor any of the other pitchers involved in arbitration were in Sutter's class as a pitcher.

Finally, look at the salary situation in pro baseball.

Baseball salaries have been skyrocketing the past few years. In just two years the average major league salary nearly doubled, from $51,000 in 1976 to $99,000 in 1978. Last year the average rose to $113,000 and you can expect it to hit close to $130,000 this year. Your own payroll averaged about $104,000 last season. Considering how few top players you have, your Cubs could not be accused of being overly stingy with their money.

Your top offer to Sutter in contract negotiations is about half of the $700,000 that your pitcher expects. Remember, though, that if the matter goes to binding arbitration, the judge must choose one figure or the other. If you make a mistake in your calculations, it would be better to be a few dollars too high in your offer. If you are a few dollars too low, the judge will be forced to settle for Sutter's huge number.

What's Your Decision?

> It's your team.
>
> This is your last chance to work out a settlement with Sutter before binding arbitration. What will you do?
>
> **#1** Go to arbitration with an offer of $350,000 for one year.
>
> **#2** Go to arbitration with an offer of $500,000 for one year.
>
> **#3** Offer Sutter a secure, long-term contract at somewhere over $600,000 per year.
>
> **#4** Give Sutter what he wants, $700,000 for the year.

Choose your strategy. Then turn the page to see what the Cubs' owner did.

The Cubs went with choice #1.

The Cubs were convinced that Sutter's demand of $700,000 for a year was ridiculous. Salaries may have been escalating, but they weren't shooting up that fast. They considered their offer of $350,000 to be a fair one, and they would stand by it in arbitration.

Here's What Happened!

The arbitrator did not think either figure was particularly fair. After studying the situation though, he concluded that Sutter's number was closer to what he deserved than the Cubs' offer. The Cubs blundered, then, by submitting too low a number. Had they sent in a final offer of $500,000, there was a much better chance that they would have won the case and they could have saved themselves $200,000.

Some baseball experts pointed out that the Cubs might have done even better by offering Sutter a long-term contract. Given the rate at which salaries were zooming, a salary that seemed high in 1979 might be a bargain in 1983. Sutter might have been tempted to go for the security of a long-term contract at slightly less salary than what he was asking for one year. As it happened, free agents such as Nolan Ryan and Goose Gossage signed enormous contracts which quickly boosted Sutter's value to well over $1 million per year.

The Cubs, feeling they couldn't afford to keep pace with the price tag on their ace reliever, were forced to trade him to the St. Louis Cardinals. There Sutter continued to baffle hitters as he led the National League in saves again in 1980, pitched the Cards to a World Series title in 1982, and recorded an incredible 45 saves in 1984.

The Cubs were able to salvage something from the situation, however. One of the players they received from the Cardinals in the Sutter trade was power hitter Leon Durham. Leon contributed a .279 average and 23 home runs to the Cubs' surprising divisional title in 1984. All factors considered, however, Chicago probably would have come out better had they taken a different approach in their contract dispute of 1980.

Sutter's success with the Cardinals raised his value even higher. In 1984 the Atlanta Braves signed him away from the Cardinals for $10 million over 6 years.

4 Curse of the Hitless Wonders

Chicago's Comiskey Park has been a pitcher's paradise over the years. All those zeros on the scoreboard are starting to put your fans to sleep.

You own the Chicago White Sox.

Ever since Chicago's "Hitless Wonders" swept to a World Series championship in 1906 despite a team batting average of only .230, your White Sox have had trouble getting runs. Even in their best years, it has been excellent pitching and fielding which has carried the club to victory, while the hitters gasped for every run they could get.

Going into the 1977 season, the problem has only gotten worse. Last year your batters were lucky to hit the ball out of the infield. When the pitching went sour as well, your team collapsed in a heap. With a 64-97 record and no offense to break the tedium, White Sox attendance dipped below a million fans. As one of the league's least wealthy teams, you can't afford to keep losing fans. What will you do?

39

First, consider just how bad it was last year.

Your White Sox showed about as much explosiveness last season as a soggy book of matches. Your top "sluggers" last year were Jim Spencer and Jorge Orta, both of whom hit 14 home runs. No one else on the team hit homers in double figures. Altogether, Chicago hit 73 home runs for the entire year, and they treated their home crowd to a grand total of 31. That averages out to about one every two and a half games. Little wonder, then, that your team scored only 586 runs to rank 10th of the 12 American League teams in that department.

Jim Spencer

Your pitching staff, meanwhile, would have been happy with that ranking. They were riddled for 745 runs or an average of 4.25 earned runs per game to rank dead last in the league. One of the worst experiments in recent baseball times was the Sox plan to turn ace relief pitchers Rich Gossage and Terry Forster into starters. Gossage responded by more than doubling his ERA (from 1.84 in 1975 to 3.94 in 1976) on his way to a nightmarish 9-17 record. Forster also doubled his ERA (from 2.19 in 1975 to 4.38 in 1976) while posting a 2-12 mark. The rest of your pitchers, with the exception of fading knuckleballer Wilbur Wood, are all young and untested.

Rich Gossage

Terry Forster

The one bright note in your season had to have been your fielding. In typical White Sox fashion, your glovemen kept mistakes to a minimum as they led the American League West in fielding percentage. Think of what would have happened to your pitchers if they hadn't benefited from that defense!

Jorge Orta's .274 average and 14 home runs were not eye-popping figures but they were good enough to make him the Sox' offensive star in 1976.

Now, consider how you can bring your fans a more entertaining team this season.

One thing you might consider is moving the outfield fences in closer at your home field. Part of the White Sox problem in hitting home runs over the years is that your Comiskey Park fences are the hardest for American League batters to reach. The foul lines in all other parks range from 302 feet (in Boston) to 340 (in Detroit). Your foul pole sits 352 feet from home plate. While your "power alleys" in left-center and right-center are about average for the league, your center field fence stretches all the way out to 440 feet. This is 20 to 40 feet beyond that of most of the other parks.

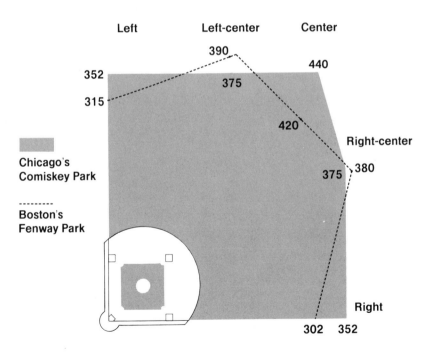

43

Moving in the fences would certainly liven up White Sox games and might attract more fans. It might, however, be a risky move. For one thing, your pitchers are having enough trouble getting batters out. What little confidence they have could be destroyed if you start turning fly ball outs into home runs.

Another point to consider is that opposing teams may be better suited than your White Sox to take advantage of the move. Closer fences are likely to help power hitters, who hit a great number of fly balls that are caught deep in the outfield. Your team just doesn't have many proven power hitters.

You might consider changing your image from the old hitless wonders to a hard-hitting team. To do that, you would have to sacrifice some fielding as well as what little pitching you have. But if you traded for some power hitters and then filled your line-up with the best hitters you had regardless of how they fielded, you would get a more explosive offense that would entertain fans.

Some experts, though, say that the best way to draw fans is simply by winning. They also add that you need pitching and defense to win. If you followed their advice, you would hang on to your Hitless Wonder image. You might have a better chance of a winning season by simply returning Gossage and Forster to the bullpen and letting your young pitching talent develop. The problem with that, of course, is that it does nothing to bolster your sleep-inducing offense.

What's Your Decision?

> It's your team.
>
> The bills are coming into your office faster than you can pay them. What will you do to get fans back to the park?
>
> **#1** Sacrifice pitching and defense; load up with power hitters.
>
> **#2** Move the fences in to provide more home runs.
>
> **#3** Try to build on your fielding and young pitching talent to get a winning team.
>
> **#4** Sell the team to someone who has the money to sign big name free agents.

Choose your strategy. Then turn the page to see what the White Sox' owner did.

The White Sox chose to go with #1.

Chicago owner Bill Veeck believed that the first rule of baseball was that the game should be fun. In his opinion, White Sox fans would get a bigger kick out of a free-swinging, fence-busting, run-scoring team than they would a bunch of defensive scrappers.

Although it was true that Comiskey Park's huge outfield cut down some on home runs, the White Sox chose not to go to the trouble of bringing in the fences. They figured that fans would appreciate an increase in the number of line-drive hits and towering home runs than they would an increase in the number of "cheap" home runs.

Before the start of the 1977 season, Chicago made a flurry of moves to supercharge their offense. They traded Gossage and Forster to the Pittsburgh Pirates for hard-hitting Richie Zisk. The Sox then peddled their steady shortstop, Bucky Dent, to the Yankees for home-run specialist Oscar Gamble. Veeck signed a lesser-known free agent, Eric Soderholm, an offensive-minded third baseman, and let big Lamar Johnson alternate with Jim Spencer at first base. Finally, .300-hitter Jorge Orta was moved from the outfield to second base, another case of sacrificing fielding for hitting.

Here's What Happened!

Within weeks of opening day, the White Sox had shredded their old hitless image. Midway into the season, Chicago streaked into first place in the American League West and fought for the lead clear into September. The hot hitting of newcomers like Zisk and Gamble seemed to rub off on the other players until the Sox attack was full of menacing swingers. Compare the statistics of some of their key players:

PLAYER	HOMERS in 1976	HOMERS in 1977
Gamble	17	31
Zisk	21	30
Soderholm	0 (injured)	25
Lemon	4	19
Spencer	14	18
Johnson	4	18
Essian	0 (injured)	10

Without moving the fences, Chicago hitters more than doubled the club's 1976 home run total of 73 by socking 192 home runs in 1977. Their pitching staff did no better —or worse—than it had the year before (same 4.25 ERA), and Chicago's fielding percentage fell from first in their division in 1976 to sixth in 1977. But Chicago simply buried their opponents in an avalanche of runs.

Lured by the promise of an explosive attack and a winning team, more than 1,600,000 fans flocked to Comiskey Park that summer, an increase of almost 700,000. The White Sox strategy had worked far better than anyone could have dreamed.

5 The Chicago Cub Blues

You own the Chicago Cubs.

For many years now, your Chicago club has been living up to its nickname: it's been as harmless as a cub. Your 1960 Cubs were such a soft-touch on opposing schedules that it's hard to imagine that this used to be one of the game's most respected teams. But since winning three pennants in the 1930s and another one in 1945, your Cubs haven't had so much as a winning season!

It seems that you've spent years trying to carefully, cautiously put together a pennant contender. But the honest truth is that your team is going nowhere. Can you come up with a bold plan that can put your team back in the pennant chase in 1961?

First, look at the history of leadership your team has had.

You've tried the standard routine of firing and hiring managers. Since that 1946 season, there's been a steady parade of men taking over the job. Frankie Frisch took over in 1949, Phil Cavaretta in 1951, ex-Cub hero Stan Hack in 1954, Bob Scheffing in 1957, Charlie Grimm and then Lou Boudreau last season.

Each of them had a chance to bring about improvement and none of them did. Could it be that it doesn't really matter who manages, that the problem is somewhere else? Or have you been such a poor judge of character that you've never chosen a good manager? After all, except for Grimm, none of these men ever enjoyed success at managing. Frisch and Boudreau had the most luck and each of them managed one pennant-winner in 16 years of trying.

The most successful manager in baseball history just happens to be available right now. The Yankees recently fired Casey Stengel, even though he directed the team to the American League championship for the 10th time in the past 12 years. If any man can manage your team to victory, it ought to be Casey. Or was it just that he always had better players than anyone else? Remember, too, that Casey is now 70 years old and has taken some criticism for his handling of pitchers in the Yankees' recent World Series loss to the Pirates.

Since 1949, Casey Stengel has won 10 pennants and 7 World Series. During that time your Cubs haven't won any. Maybe he knows something you don't.

Now take an honest look at the talent on your team.

It hasn't been luck that has caused your Cubs to hover around the bottom of the standings; they've earned their losing records. If it weren't for Ernie Banks, the National League would have an awful time trying to select a player to represent the Cubs at the All-Star game. Banks is a cheerful, popular shortstop who has starred for the team since 1954. He has single-handedly carried the Cub offense for years, especially when he hit .313 with a league-leading 47 home runs in 1958. At 30 years of age, he is in his prime, as he showed again last season by leading the National League in home runs.

Ernie Banks

Richie Ashburn, acquired in a trade from Philadelphia, can still hit .300 but is slowing down in the outfield. Don Elston has shown ability as a relief pitcher. Other than that, there's not much to brag about.

Your minor league system, however, seems to be full of good, young prospects. Lou Brock, Ken Hobbs, Paul Popovich, and Billy Williams are a few of the raw recruits who may someday make a name for themselves in the majors.

What's Your Decision?

It's your team.
You're losing fans, you have no manager, and you have few polished big league players. It's time for some drastic action. What will you do?

#1 Hire Casey Stengel as manager.

#2 Instead of hiring a manager, hire a large group of baseball instructors to run the team and develop your young talent.

#3 Hire a young manager and then stockpile talent for the future by trading Banks for more exciting young prospects to add to the ones you already have.

#4 Hire the popular Banks as player/manager. At the same time, trade your talented younger players for established stars who can help you win now.

Choose your strategy. Then turn the page to find out what the Cubs did.

The Cubs went with choice #2.

Owner Phil Wrigley decided to try out a brand new idea, which was called the College of Coaches. He reasoned that his young players would have the best chance of developing if he could provide them with the best instruction possible. Therefore, he hired a group of coaches who could work together to develop a learning program that would improve the Cubs' play. Rather than appoint one of them manager, Wrigley wanted to make each of them feel he was an important part of the operation, and so they were all to share the job of manager.

The Cubs certainly didn't want to trade their most popular player (#4) nor distract his play by making him player/manager (#3). The 70-year old Stengel was not seriously considered for the job (#1).

Here's What Happened!

Under the direction of their eight specialists, Chicago improved its performance by four games in 1961, finishing with a 64-90 mark. Determined to at least give the idea a chance, the Cubs added three more coaches for 1962. Unfortunately, the "musical coaches" experiment, as the press ridiculed it, was a disaster. Despite the addition of two woefully weak expansion clubs to their schedule, the Cubs actually slipped to a 59-103 mark. The only team the Cubs beat in the standings that year was the New York Mets, who set a major league record for losses in a season. Besides being unproductive, the College of Coaches cost a small fortune. After paying out a million dollars in salaries and expenses for his instructors only to see no improvement, owner Phil Wrigley went back to the one-manager system in 1963.

Although it was certainly a good idea to bring instruction to the young players, the Cubs' disastrous record indicated that things do not run smoothly when there are too many leaders. Supporting the theory that there is only room for one at the top, new manager Bob Kennedy took over from the coaches and immediately led the Cubs to its first winning season since 1946. Since that time, no other team has been tempted to try the Cubs' multiple manager plan.

6 Buy Now, Pay Later

Hoyt Wilhelm can bring fast relief to your Braves, with the bill to be paid later. But how high will that bill be?

You own the Atlanta Braves.

This 1969 race for the National League West championship could be the wildest in history. With less than a
month to go in the season, five of the six divisional teams
are wrestling for the lead. It's a rare opportunity for
your Braves. You want to make sure you do all you
can to claim your first championship since 1958.

You've just found out that the California Angels are
interested in trading their ace relief pitcher, Hoyt Wilhelm.
Your bullpen isn't the best in the league but neither
is it the worst. What is it worth to you to get Wilhelm?

Look over your scouting report on the granddaddy of modern relief pitchers.

There has never been a relief pitcher like Hoyt Wilhelm. Back in 1952, Hoyt became the first reliever ever to win an ERA title. In the 17 seasons since then, his fluttering knuckleball has had batters grinding their teeth in frustration. No relief pitcher can come close to matching Hoyt's records of nearly 1,000 appearances, over 200 saves, and more than 130 career wins.

Of course, Wilhelm is 46 years old, but his knuckler is thrown with such an easy motion that he may last until he's 50. From 1964 to 1968, Hoyt showed no signs of slowing down as he kept his earned run average below 2.00. This season he has slipped a touch, with a 5-7 record, 10 saves, and a 2.47 ERA for the Angels.

Now mull over what the Angels are asking in return.

California has no hope of a winning record this season, and so they are building for the future. They are willing to offer you a "buy now—pay later" deal. In exchange for Wilhelm, you would not have to lose a single player from your major league roster. Instead, California would like to choose one of your better minor league prospects.

The man they have their eye on is center fielder Mickey Rivers. Mickey is a fine athlete with scorching speed, but he is just starting on the road to a major league career. It will probably be two or three years before he's ready to handle major league pitching. With his great speed, though, he has a good chance to be a valuable player in a key defensive position once he develops.

Finally, weigh your chances of winning this title without Wilhelm.

	Wins	Losses	Games Behind
Cincinnati	76	61	—
San Francisco	77	63	½
Los Angeles	74	63	2
Atlanta	76	65	2
Houston	73	65	3½

You have been getting good relief pitching from Cecil Upshaw, who has saved or won more than 30 games this season. If you could get some better work from your starting pitchers, you probably wouldn't give a second thought to your bullpen needs. Unfortunately, Phil Niekro is the only starter who can get by without relief help. That's meant that Upshaw has had to throw a lot of pressure-packed pitches lately.

Play-off tension can take its toll on an overworked reliever. Will Upshaw hold up under the strain or will he self-destruct?

Cecil Upshaw

Phil Niekro

What's Your Decision?

It's your team.
The race is so close that a single player could make the difference. Will you sacrifice a possible star of the future for a 46-year old pitcher? What will you do?

#1 Make the trade for Wilhelm.

#2 Keep Rivers and count on Upshaw.

Choose your strategy. Then turn the page to find out what the Braves did.

The Atlanta Braves elected to make the trade (#1).

It wasn't often that the Braves had a genuine chance to win a championship. Atlanta reasoned that it would be foolish to let the opportunity get away while they saved up for the future. It made no sense to gamble on an overworked Upshaw carrying the load alone when help was available. They felt that Wilhelm could definitely help their team, especially since they could get him without giving up anyone on their major league roster.

Here's What Happened!

Shortly after joining the team, Wilhelm was called in to finish a close game against the Giants. Hoyt breezed through the ninth inning to record the save which put the Braves into a tie for first with the Reds. One day later, Wilhelm saved a game with the Astros to give his team sole possession of first place. Then, pitching for the third day in a row, tireless Hoyt collected a win as Atlanta moved out to a 1½ game lead over the pack.

Wilhelm went on to win two more games and save two others as the Braves roared to 17 wins in their last 21 games. Each of Hoyt's contributions was crucial as the Braves edged the Giants for the title by three games. Wilhelm's value to Atlanta was proven in the play-offs. He had joined the club too late in the season to qualify for the post-season action. Without Wilhelm to come to the rescue, the Braves pitchers were pounded by the Mets and eliminated in a three-game romp.

Rivers, meanwhile, spent four years bouncing from the minors to the majors before winning a starting job in 1974. Once he got used to big league pitching, though, he became a fine and exciting player. Atlanta stumbled through the 1970s without an exceptional centerfielder while their ex-minor leaguer hit for high average, stole bases, and chased down fly balls for other teams. Had the Wilhelm trade not helped the Braves win their 1969 title, there would have been many regrets about the deal. But the Braves were satisfied that, as in most trades, you have to give something to get something.

Wilhelm walks to the mound to snuff out a Cardinal rally. His knuckleball carried the Braves to first place in one of the closest divisional races in history.

7 Room for an Ancient Mariner?

Gaylord began pitching for the Giants 297 wins ago. Will you give him the chance to reach the magic 300?

You own the Seattle Mariners.

The Mariners' five-year plan for moving from expansion castoffs to pennant contender has fizzled badly. After another miserable record in 1981, the year of the strike, you're right back where you started. Your (44-65) mark kept alive your sad streak of never finishing higher than sixth in your division.

With your team going nowhere, you have to rebuild almost from scratch. It will take patience to develop your young players into a winning outfit. Unfortunately, your disappointed fans don't have much patience left.

Suddenly, you've received a call from Gaylord Perry. This ancient pitching star is looking for a job and hasn't found any takers. Do you want to take a chance on him?

Review the pitching record of this aging right-hander.

Throughout his 20 years of major league play, Perry has either been the best spitball pitcher or the best bluffer in the game. Although no one has ever caught him serving up an illegal spitball, Perry seems to know how to make a ball do strange tricks. As a result, he has won a Cy Young Award as the league's best pitcher in both the American and National Leagues.

He first claimed that award in 1972, when he won 24 and lost 16 with a sparkling 1.92 ERA for the Cleveland Indians. Six years later, after most baseball experts had considered him washed up, Gaylord's 21-6 record for the lowly San Diego Padres earned him the National League Cy Young.

Perry is creeping up on two milestones that would guarantee him a spot in baseball's Hall of Fame. First, he is within sight of the great Walter Johnson's major league strikeout mark. Secondly, with 297 career victories, Perry has a chance to become pro baseball's first 300-game winner since 1963.

San Diego took a chance on the "old-timer" in 1978 and he rewarded them with a 21-6 record.

Look at Perry's most recent marks to see if he can still pitch.

Gaylord is well past the age when he was supposed to have retired. You can count on one hand the number of 43-year old hurlers who can still get big league batters out. And, with at least 220 pounds covering his 6-foot, 4-inch frame, Perry doesn't appear to be in terrific physical shape. The ex-star has had to scramble to keep his spot on the roster the past few years. As a result, he has bounced around from San Diego to Texas to New York to Atlanta and now to the unemployment lines. Not one of the other 25 teams in the majors has shown any interest in Perry this spring.

During this past season, though, he pitched respectably for the Atlanta Braves. His 1981 mark of 8 wins, 9 losses, 3.93 ERA, while not outstanding, is nothing to laugh at. Remember, too, that Perry has been one of the most durable pitchers in history, missing only two starts during his long career.

Perry has worn many hats during his career. As fast as one team has given up on him, someone else has given him a try.

Finally, consider the effect that Perry would have on your ball club.

There is no doubt that your pitching staff needs emergency first aid. The top man on the Seattle staff last year was Floyd Bannister, who won only nine games during the strike-shortened season. And Bannister's meager win total was more than twice what any of your other starters earned! The Mariners' team ERA of 4.23 was by far the worst in the American League. In only 10 of Seattle's 109 games last year did the starting pitcher stick around for the finish.

With many of your top young prospects either injured or struggling, things don't look any brighter for 1982. Bannister will be back to lead the staff, and you hope that 27-year old Jim Beattie can be an effective second starter. But beyond that there's no one you can count on. If Perry can put together a season like he did in Atlanta last year, he would certainly be at least the third best starting pitcher on your team.

A new pitcher, though brings more than just a record with him; he also brings his personality. You have a young team that needs to develop confidence, and the word around the league is that Gaylord can be murder on young players, especially fielders who make errors. He's a tough competitor, known for needling youngsters to see if they can take it. Some managers consider Perry to be a problem player. They remember very clearly how he quit the San Diego team near the end of the 1979 season when they wouldn't trade him to a team nearer his North Carolina farm.

A final factor to consider is attendance. Your Mariners drew only 636,276 last season, second worst in the American League. Perry's fight to reach the exclusive 300-win club would certainly receive national coverage and your club could use any attention it can get. There's a chance that sell-out crowds might cram the Kingdome to see old Gaylord go after that milestone. The boost in attendance could easily offset Perry's high salary, which has discouraged other teams from signing him.

What's Your Decision?

It's your team.

Perry is waiting for an answer from you. Can he shore up your pitching staff or will he be more trouble than he's worth? What will you do?

#1 Sign him to a one-year contract.

#2 Go with youth to rebuild your team and stay away from Perry.

#3 Ask him to join your team on a month-by-month trial basis.

Choose your strategy. Then turn the page to see what the Mariners' management did.

Seattle went with option #3.

Seattle thought it likely that Perry could improve their pitching staff and boost their attendance but they didn't want to commit themselves to paying Perry's way for a whole year. If it turned out that the 43-year old couldn't pitch anymore, they didn't want to be stuck with him. Perry realized that his long career was in danger. Being so close to reaching some fantastic goals, he was more interested in playing than in quibbling about salary. The old master signed with Seattle, confident they would be happy with his performance.

Here's What Happened!

Seattle's hope of cashing in on Perry's 300th win didn't pan out. Fewer than 28,000 fans showed up to watch Gaylord's historic moment, a 7-3 victory over the New York Yankees. By comparison, a "funny nose/glasses" promotion just two nights later attracted nearly 37,000!

Perry more than made up for that disappointment, though, with his performance both on and off the field. Posting a 10-2 record in games in which his team scored four runs or more, Gaylord finished with a respectable 10-12 record, including six complete games.

Even at age 43, Gaylord stayed a leg up on his opponents.

Not only did he fill a desperate need for the Mariners on the mound, he surprised them with his steadying influence on younger players. Far from the bitter, ornery, selfish man he had been painted as, Gaylord patiently showed his teammates how to win in the big leagues. Young pitchers such as Bannister, Bill Caudill, and Ed Vande Berg pitched superbly that season. Seattle's team ERA dropped to 3.88, the fourth best mark in the American League. That improvement showed up in the standings, where Seattle posted their best record ever, 76-86. It also showed up in paid attendance, which climbed to 1,070,404. The decision to sign Perry turned out even better than the Mariners had expected.

8 A Disastrous Start

You own the Atlanta Braves.

It hasn't been easy breaking the Braves of their long losing tradition. You've worked overtime and have gone through a large chunk of your life savings in scouting, trading, and buying players, and in signing top free agents. After four straight last place finishes, this 1980 season is supposed to be the year when it starts to pay off in victories.

Instead, your Braves have started off the year by falling flat on their noses. Even your worst teams of the past few years haven't opened the season with only one win in ten games the way this team has. What will you do?

Evaluate your team's strengths and weaknesses.

You've worked hard to beef up your hitting. Now you have a lineup that reminds fans of the old days when Hank Aaron and Eddie Matthews rained home runs on the outfield bleachers. Most teams would feel comfortable with two proven sluggers in their batting order; you have <u>five</u> of these fence-busters.

It cost you plenty to sign free agent outfielder Gary Matthews away from the San Francisco Giants, but he has been worth it. Last season he hit .304, with 27 home runs. Joining him in the outfield this season are Dale Murphy and Jeff Burroughs. Young Murphy is already being labeled a star of the future. Last season he just tapped the surface of his great potential with a .276 average and 21 homers. Burroughs seems to have temporarily lost his hitting touch as he swatted only 11 home runs last year while batting .224. But once he gets the bugs worked out of his swing, he could regain the form that won the American League's Most Valuable Player Award in 1974 and that smacked 41 home runs for you in 1977.

The powerful threesome of Gary Matthews, Dale Murphy, and Jeff Burroughs is hardly your typical last-place outfield.

Third base is the fielding home of your hottest prospect of all, Bob Horner. In his first full season of major league ball, Horner drilled 33 home runs while batting .314. On the other side of the infield, newcomer Chris Chambliss brings his dangerous bat over from the New York Yankees. Chambliss has consistently hit around .280 with 15-20 home runs during his career.

Chris Chambliss

Bob Horner

Atlanta's power, though, has often been canceled by weak pitching. Whenever anyone has anything nice to say about your pitching staff, you know they're talking about knuckleball ace Phil Niekro. The tireless Niekro is good for 300 innings of sound hurling every year. In 1979, however, none of your other pitchers won more than eight games. This season there are a lot of new faces on the staff, but still no proven starters to help Niekro. Your strategy is mainly to outslug the other team.

Gritty knuckleball artist Phil Niekro has been carrying the whole pitching load for the Braves.

Now try to determine if there are any individuals who are responsible for your poor start.

One of your better players has already pulled enough boners this year to fill a baseball follies highlight film. Third baseman Horner has amassed 6 errors in 10 games. If he continues at that rate, he has a shot at being the first major leaguer to boot 100 chances in a single year. And, although one of baseball's top hitters last year, Horner is batting a microscopic .059 so far. He may be setting a record for slow starts!

Another person who has to be on the hot seat for your poor showing is the manager. Traditionally, when a baseball team goes bad the first thing the owner does is fire the manager. Even though a poor performance may not be the fault of the manager, many baseball experts feel a drastic change of some kind is needed to jolt a club out of its losing ways. Since managers are easier to find than good ball players, it's usually easier to axe the manager than to get rid of players.

Manager Bobby Cox is widely considered an able manager. Yet his record of the past few years is shaky at best. Cox managed your Braves to a last place 69-93 mark in 1978, and slipped even further last season to 66-94 record.

Manager Bobby Cox

What's Your Decision?

It's your team.

Although it's still early in the season, you can't afford to get too far behind in the standings. With all your high-priced players, another last-place finish would be a disaster. What's your decision?

#1 Trade one or more of your sluggers for a top starting pitcher.

#2 Be patient and wait for your team to pull out of what must be just a temporary slump.

#3 Fire manager Bobby Cox.

#4 Send Horner to the minor leagues until he improves.

Choose your strategy. Then turn the page to see what the Braves did.

The Braves selected option #4.

Owner Ted Turner was not the type of person to sit around and watch his team wreck their season in the first month. He decided he needed to shake up the team. Going against the normal procedures of baseball, he supported his manager, Bobby Cox, and went after Horner instead. He hoped that sending Horner down to the Braves' minor league team at Richmond would jolt both Horner and other Braves into giving a more complete effort.

Owner Ted Turner (baseball cap) has never been afraid of controversy. His decision to send Bob Horner packing jolted the Braves, and made Horner furious.

Here's What Happened!

Turner's action certainly jolted Horner, who considered the demotion to be the worst insult that could be given to him. He refused to report to Richmond and that touched off a bitter squabble between the star and the owner. Atlanta suspended their third baseman and threatened him with a $2,000 a day loss in wages if he wouldn't report. Horner, in turn, filed a grievance against the Braves. In it, he claimed that the Braves' move violated his contract, and he asked to be declared a free agent.

The Braves, meanwhile, seemed to respond to the action. They won four games in a row immediately after Horner's suspension. Those wins, though, came about as a result of a few rare, sparkling pitching performances. Atlanta then lost five of their next eight games and were still in last place when Horner was allowed back on the team three weeks later.

When the still-smoldering Horner returned to the line-up, he took out his frustrations on opposing pitchers. Proving that he did not belong in the minor leagues, Horner blasted 35 home runs in the last four months of the season. Atlanta recovered from their slow start to post a winning record, 81-80, as they climbed out of last place at last.

Was Turner's move responsible for the improvement of Horner and the Braves? Or, given their great talent, would they gradually have gotten into the winning groove anyway? Neither case can be proven. Yet, given the risk of losing a fine player, and the hassles and hostility that went with this decision, it will probably be a long time before an owner tries to make a move like that again.

9 A Major Player Shuffle

You own the Detroit Tigers.

It's World Series time, 1970. You would like to relax, enjoy the contest between Cincinnati and Baltimore, and forget about the losing season your once-powerful Tigers just finished. Your hopes for a brief vacation, however, have been quickly dashed. The Washington Senators' aggressive new owner, Robert Short, is out to improve his ball club and one man he wants is your pitcher Denny McLain.

The more you talk to Short, the more complicated the deal becomes. The way things stand now, eight or nine players could be involved. In a whopping trade like this one, you want to make sure you don't overlook any of the details. Will you trade with the Senators or not?

Here's the way the proposed trade looks.

You will give up:

McLain, pitcher Norm McRae, third baseman Don Wert, and all-purpose utilityman Elliot Maddox. Washington is also pushing hard to get you to add reserve infielder Ike Brown to the deal.

In exchange, you will receive:

Pitchers Joe Coleman and Jim Hannan, shortstop Eddie Brinkman, and third baseman Aurelio Rodriguez.

Here's a scouting report on each player.

DETROIT TIGERS

Denny McLain

Since 1965, Denny has probably been the best pitcher in baseball. After winning 20 games in 1966, McLain mowed down opposing batters to post a fantastic 31-6 record with a 1.96 ERA in 1968. He followed that in 1969 by hurling nine shutouts while topping the American League in wins for the second time with 24.

Despite these totals, McLain has been anything but a joy to work with. Your star got himself so deeply in debt that he had to declare bankruptcy. This past season he was suspended by the commissioner of baseball for a total of 71 games when it was discovered he was involved in a gambling operation. A sore pitching arm, which has been bothering him off and on for years, acted up again when he finally joined the team in July. As a result he won only three games and lost five for you this past year.

McLain is the key player in the deal. Washington would like him because they feel they need a big-name star around which to build their struggling team.

Don Wert

A good fielder but a poor hitter, Wert has been in the majors since 1963. During the past three years, he has batted no higher than .225.

Norm McRae

A newcomer to the big leagues, McRae pitched only 31 innings last year with no wins or losses.

Elliot Maddox

Another man fresh up from the minors, Maddox batted .248 with 3 home runs last season in limited playing time. He is a potential starter who the scouts feel can hit .300 in the big leagues.

Ike Brown

Brown is not a good fielder but hit .287 with 4 home runs in just 94 at bats in 1970, his second year with Detroit.

Don Wert

Norm McRae

Elliott Maddox

Ike Brown

Denny McLain

Joe Coleman

Eddie Brinkman

Aurelio Rodriguez

Jim Hannan

Joe Coleman

A six-year veteran, Coleman won 8 and lost 12 last year, with a 3.58 ERA. Considering that he played for a poor team, that's not a bad mark. He's the man who would have to replace McLain as one of your starting pitchers.

Eddie Brinkman

Since 1961, Brinkman has been the classic example of the "good field, no hit" shortstop. His fielding has been spectacular enough to win a starting job most of those years even though he has trouble hitting his weight.

Aurelio Rodriguez

Along with Brinkman, third baseman Rodriguez could patch up your shaky defense on the left side of the infield. Aurelio, a four-year veteran, is a fair hitter who can also belt a home run from time to time. Last season he hit 19 homers with a .249 average.

Jim Hannan

Hannan, who can either start or relieve, has played in the majors since 1962. His statistics for last year were similar to Coleman's: 9-11, 4.01 ERA. Unlike Coleman, however, Hannan has probably reached his peak as a pitcher.

What's Your Decision?

It's your team.

Baseball owners can change their minds from day to day. Before someone makes Short a better offer, you'll have to decide whether or not this trade will help your ball club. What will you do?

#1 Agree to trade McLain, Wert, Maddox, McRae, and Brown for Coleman, Brinkman, Rodriguez, and Hannan.

#2 Agree to trade only McLain, Wert, Maddox, and McRae for the four Senators. Refuse to give them Brown.

#3 Turn down the trade.

Make your decision. Then turn the page to see what the Tigers did.

The Tigers went with choice number #2.

Detroit felt that Washington was so eager to get a big-name star like McLain that they wouldn't haggle over a marginal player such as Brown. With all the problems McLain had been having, Detroit was actually glad for a chance to trade him. They figured that Coleman might not be as good a pitcher as McLain had once been, but he was healthier. Rodriguez and Brinkman were easily more valuable than Wert and Maddox. Hannan and McRae were just throw-ins who had no real effect on the deal.

Here's What Happened!

A baseball expert named Bill James evaluated all baseball trades made between 1963 and 1973, and assigned a number to illustrate the value of each player to his new team. In this deal, James gave the new Tigers a value of 115 and the new Senators 14, making it the most one-sided trade of the decade. Many experts point to this deal as the one which ruined the Senators, disgusted their fans, and forced them to move to Texas.

Coleman stepped right in to become the ace of the Tiger staff as he won 20 games in 1971, 19 in 1972, and 23 in 1973. Brinkman improved the Tiger defense at the crucial shortstop position, starting there for four years. Rodriguez provided steady third base play and timely, if unspectacular, hitting for the next eight years.

What happened to the players they gave up? Ex-star McLain skidded to a 10-22 mark with a 4.27 ERA in 1971. In the process he hurt his arm and never pitched effectively again. Wert managed only 2 hits in 40 at bats and didn't last three months with the Senators. Maddox played sparingly and poorly for the Senators for three seasons before being sold to the Yankees. Neither McRae nor Hannan pitched effectively at all after the trade.

One of the puzzles of the deal was why Detroit risked blowing the trade for the sake of Ike Brown. Brown rarely saw action over the next few seasons and retired without making much of a name for himself. Even if they had included Brown in the deal, it would have ranked as one of the biggest steals in baseball history.

10 A Costly Blunder

Dave Kingman misses by a mile again. You paid $700,000
to see him strike out?

You own the New York Mets.

National sports magazines have just declared that the surest thing in baseball is that your Mets will finish last in 1984. After some of the moves your management has pulled lately, that's not surprising. The worst of those brainstorms was the decision made a few years ago to sign Dave Kingman to a multi-year contract at an enormous salary. Now it turns out that Kingman can't crack into your starting lineup.

You've tried to trade this ex-home run champ but can't get any offers for him. That means you are really stuck. Even if Kingman never puts on a Mets uniform this season, his contract guarantees that you will pay him $700,000. How do you get out of this mess?

Look at Kingman's record to see if there's any way that he can help the Mets this season.

It's incredible that a player's value could drop so suddenly. Nearly every team is looking for a right-handed power hitter, and Kingman has been one of the best. Only three players currently active in the majors have hit more career homers than Kingman! As recently as 1982, this 6-foot, 6-inch slugger led the National League in home runs with 37.

One of Dave's problems, though, is that he rarely hits anything but home runs. His 1982 batting average of .204 was the lowest ever for a home-run champ. And unfortunately, his glove work on first base or in the outfield does not sparkle at all.

Last season Kingman was mired in a deep slump when St. Louis offered to trade you Keith Hernandez. You took them up on the offer and obtained the slick-fielding, clutch-hitting first baseman. But the Hernandez trade bumped the struggling Kingman off first base. The outfield was already filled with three solid starters, Darryl Strawberry, Mookie Wilson, and George Foster, so that left Kingman on the bench.

Dave started only six games and hit only one home run during the last half of the year. He totaled only 13 home runs and a .194 batting average that year. Those are poor numbers for a poor-fielding, 35-year old with a $700,000-a-year salary. No wonder no one is interested.

Mookie Wilson (top left), Darryl Strawberry (top right), and
George Foster (bottom) give you a solid outfield. With first
base already occupied by All-Star Keith Hernandez, there
seems to be no room left for Kingman.

Now, go over the few options that you have.

The simplest thing to do is to swallow hard and give Kingman his release. True, you will still have to shell out $700,000 to him. But if the man isn't going to help you, why pay him just to take up space on your roster? Wouldn't your team be better off if you admitted you made a mistake and replaced Kingman with someone who could help you?

On the other hand, what if Kingman then signs with another team in your division? If he is released and not traded, you would still be responsible for his salary. If he should somehow return to his old form, you might get caught in the awkward position of paying most of his salary while he beats you out of a pennant!

Another possibility would be to keep him as a pinch hitter and spot starter. Remember that your Mets scored 48 fewer runs than any other National League team in 1983 and ranked last in slugging percentage. Kingman may not have done much else for you last year, but he still hit 13 homers in only 248 at bats. If you take away his bat your Mets will be even shorter on offensive power than they already were.

Many power hitters, however, need to play often to be effective. Kingman's weak production as a reserve in the last half of the season may be proof that he can't help as a pinch hitter. That brings up a third possibility. Put Kingman in the regular lineup for a month or two and see how he does. If he gets into the hitting groove and shows that he can still belt home runs, other teams will become interested in him. Then you'll be able to trade him for a player you can really use.

There are two disadvantages to this last option: 1) by playing Kingman in place of Wilson, Foster, Strawberry, or Hernandez, you won't have your best team on the field, and 2) Kingman may not do any better than he did last year.

What's Your Decision?

It's your team.
You're stuck with Kingman's $700,000 salary, but what will you do with Kingman?

#1 Give him his release.

#2 Keep him as a reserve.

#3 Play him regularly and try to increase his trade value.

Choose your strategy. Then turn the page to see what the Mets did.

The Mets settled for option #1.

The Mets were convinced that Kingman couldn't help them. Based on last year's performance, they didn't think Dave would be of much value as a reserve, and he certainly wasn't good enough to move Hernandez or the outfielders out of their starting positions. Apparently, no one else wanted Kingman either, so there seemed to be no point in wasting a month or two of the season trying to pretend he was still a star. The Mets could see no option other than letting him go.

Here's What Happened!

The Oakland Athletics desperately needed a right-handed power hitter. As long as it didn't cost them anything, they agreed to let Kingman try to win a job with them in spring training. They were pleasantly surprised with his hitting and signed him for the season.

Dave showed that he was far from washed up. As some scouts had suspected, Kingman just needed a chance to play regularly to get his timing right. As Oakland's designated hitter, Kingman returned to his old form. With 35 home runs, Dave finished second in the American League after leading the major leagues for most of the season. His 118 runs batted in placed third in the league, and he even raised his average to a respectable .268. In one of baseball's best bargains, Oakland had to pay Kingman only the league minimum salary of $40,000 while the Mets had to cough up the rest of the $700,000.

The Mets, of course, weren't pleased that they were bankrolling another club's top offensive threat. But their decision could have turned out worse. At least Kingman was out of harm's way, hitting homers in the American League rather than for one of the Mets' National League East rivals such as the Cubs. The Mets, in fact, hardly noticed the loss of Kingman as they put together one of their best seasons in years. As long as they couldn't erase the mistake of signing Kingman to that big contract, both the Mets and Kingman were probably better off going their separate ways rather than struggling to salvage something from a bad situation.

ACKNOWLEDGMENTS

Photo Credits: Atlanta Braves, pp. 61 (both), 65, 79 (all), 80 (both), 81, 83, 84; Baltimore Orioles, p. 22; George Brace, pp. 90 (bottom), 91 (all); California Angels, pp. 15, 21 (both), 25 (both), 56; Chicago Cubs, p. 28; Chicago White Sox, pp. 38, 40, 41 (both), 42; Cincinnati Reds, p. 9 (both); Cleveland Indians, p. 71 (top left); Detroit Tigers, p. 90 (all but bottom); Independent Picture Service, p. 52; Minnesota Twins, pp. 16, 18, 26; National Baseball Hall of Fame and Museum, Inc., p. 51; New York Mets, pp. 96, 99 (all); New York Yankees, pp. 10 (both), 11, 12; St. Louis Cardinals, p. 37; San Diego Padres, pp. 69, 71 (bottom left); San Francisco Giants, pp. 66, 71 (top right); Seattle Mariners, p. 75; Texas Rangers, p. 71 (bottom right); Bob Wolfe, p. 4.

Cover photo by Michael K. Herbert

Also by Nate Aaseng

FOOTBALL: IT'S YOUR TEAM
10 sink-or-swim situations

BASEBALL: YOU ARE THE MANAGER
10 exciting championship games

BASKETBALL: YOU ARE THE COACH
10 exciting NBA play-off games

FOOTBALL: YOU ARE THE COACH
10 exciting NFL play-off games

HOCKEY: YOU ARE THE COACH
10 exciting NHL play-off and international games

COLLEGE BASKETBALL: YOU ARE THE COACH
10 exciting NCAA final four games

COLLEGE FOOTBALL: YOU ARE THE COACH
10 exciting bowl games

Lerner Publications Company
241 First Avenue North, Minneapolis, MN 55401